Ursula Kühnemann

Cold Enamelling

A modern material
for a new hobby

D1365280

Mills & Boon, London
Taplinger Co. Inc., New York

This translation first published in England 1972 by Mills & Boon Limited,
17-19 Foley Street, London WIA 1 DR

First published in the United States in 1972 by
    Taplinger Publishing Co. Inc.
    New York, New York

British ISBN 0-263-05292-3

American ISBN (Paperback) 0-8008-1685-4
American (Cloth spine) ISBN 0-8008-1684-6
Library of Congress Catalog Card Number 72-2181

Contents

This book is intended to introduce a new hobby, based on a modern material. The title embodies a generally accepted term, but in fact it is far removed from traditional enamelling, and the substance used is a synthetic liquid resin.

Epoxy resin, glass-clear or coloured, will coat almost any material. Even glass and china are suitable, as well as cardboard or metal foil or textiles.

Working the resin presents no problems. It is amazingly simple to use: apply a coat, and leave to harden. The surface will set smooth and lustrous without application of heat. All colour shades may be obtained by mixing. The attraction of the finished pieces lies in the glow and sparkle of the surface, in the shimmering depth and the translucency of the coat, and in the intermingling of colours which never ceases to fascinate, as well as in the brilliant intensity of the pigments, the striking combinations of translucent and opaque areas. It is possible to turn out some really fine things; perhaps, given taste and imagination, the antiques of tomorrow. Coating with resin is a new hobby of endless possibilities. You too will find it unexpectedly rewarding.

Wooden box. The top was coated with opaque white, to which were added translucent red and blue, and "gold" powder. A darning needle was used to draw lines from the centre to the edge. The sides of the box were stained dark red.

A PLACE TO WORK

A table with good light is required. A plastics tablecloth prevents staining, and gelled resin can be easily removed from it. The work is carried out at normal room temperature. If the room is too cold, a film will form on the mixture, but this will disappear if the mixture is slightly heated. Not too much heat should be applied, though, as the resin is mixed in a plastic container, and this must not melt.

The lacquer artists in Ancient China used to go to sea in order to practise their art in an entirely dustfree atmosphere. We do not have to go to quite such lengths. If nevertheless dust particles are discernible on the gelled surface, paint on another coat of "glass-clear". Once a fluffy mohair jumper spoiled some of my pieces. Since then I have taken care to wear only non-hairy clothes for this job.

The work table must be absolutely level; otherwise the coating will be uneven. If no spirit level is at hand to test the evenness of the surface, fill a flat dish with water, almost to the brim. The distance of the water from the rim will then show whether the table is level, or which leg should be raised.

Six pendants. Top: Blue translucent, mounted with three mosaic crystals, pink. — Blue translucent with light-blue opaque.

Centre: Light-blue opaque with blue translucent, mounted with separately moulded, glass-clear beadlets. — Blue translucent with „gold" powder, two spirals drawn with a spatula.

Below: Blue translucent with mounted mosaic stones, light-blue and white opaque. — Light-blue opaque with blue translucent.

Opposite: Various pendants. Ready-made metal blanks coated with opaque and translucent colours.

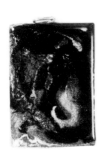

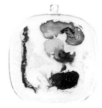

7

Pendant and ear-drops. Green translucent with light-green opaque, mounted with crystal mosaic stones in orange.

Pendant. A home-made rubber shape covered with silver mixture. The reverse was also coated. The two round pieces were cast separately on templates, yellowish-green and green translucent, and fitted subsequently.

A deceptively precious-looking pendant. A garden pebble, coated green translucent with turquoise opaque.

2

THE TOOLS

The most important tool is a pointed spatula. These generally have a narrow working surface at both ends.

The other tools you need will depend on what you want to do. For example:

A brush to draw outlines

Tweezers to remove fluff

Jewellers' pliers to attach links and chains

A wire-cutter to cut out metal foil

A hand-drill to cut holes.

The "spoons" sold with some ice creams are very useful when applying and spreading larger amounts.

Disposable plastics beakers, and containers from ice cream or cottage cheese, carefully washed, may be used. The smaller the base area, the more rapidly the material will gel (unlike lacquers which dry more rapidly in a larger container).

The mixing cups may be used over and over again, as resin once hardened will not dissolve. Make sure, though, that it is hard before adding new material.

A working board is to be greatly recommended. A piece of plywood, roughly 24 x 30 cm (10 by 12 inches) in size can be obtained from do-it-yourself shops. This should then be covered with self-adhesive white plastics sheet. On this, stick strips of plastics tape adhesive on both sides. On these, place the blanks to be covered. They can be easily removed but in the meantime will not slip during treatment. They need not be touched again and can be left to harden in their own good time.

The board with the finished pieces should be taken to a safe, dustfree room until hardening is complete.

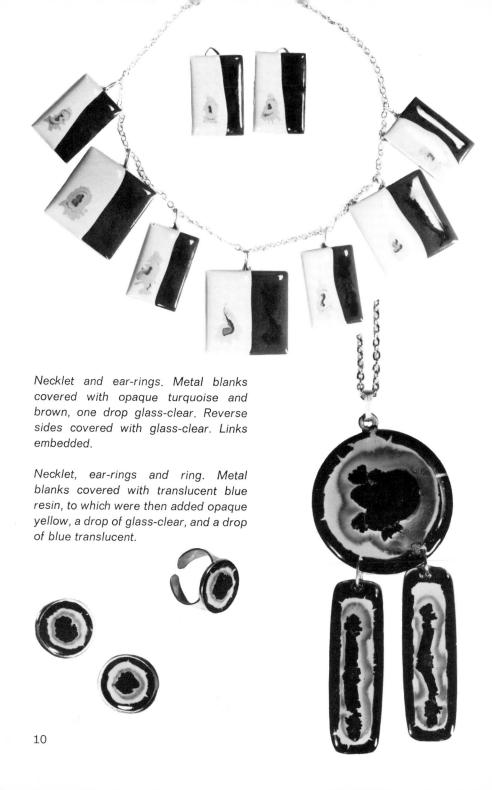

Necklet and ear-rings. Metal blanks covered with opaque turquoise and brown, one drop glass-clear. Reverse sides covered with glass-clear. Links embedded.

Necklet, ear-rings and ring. Metal blanks covered with translucent blue resin, to which were then added opaque yellow, a drop of glass-clear, and a drop of blue translucent.

Pendant for zip fastener. Red and purple opaque with "gold" dots.

Necklace and bangle.
The individual "stones" consist of forms wound round with transparent adhesive tape. Coated with translucent blue resin. Stones attached to the bangle with glue.

11

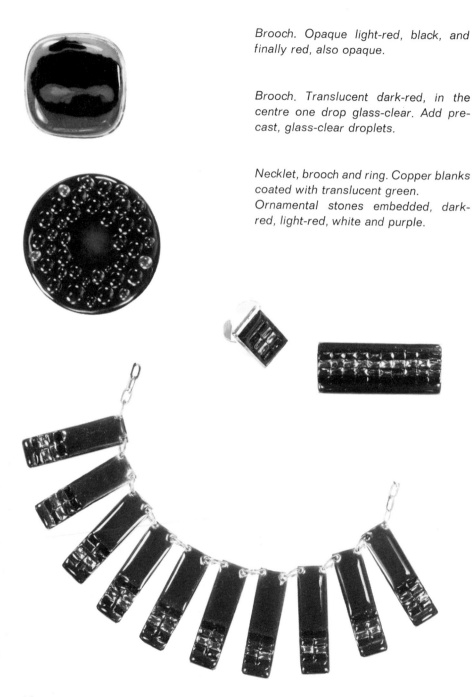

Brooch. Opaque light-red, black, and finally red, also opaque.

Brooch. Translucent dark-red, in the centre one drop glass-clear. Add pre-cast, glass-clear droplets.

Necklet, brooch and ring. Copper blanks coated with translucent green.
Ornamental stones embedded, dark-red, light-red, white and purple.

3

MATTERS TO CONSIDER

Before mixing the material, the crafts-
man should have made up his mind
about the object to be coated, the pigments to be used, the extras needed,
and any special effects he wishes to
obtain. Obviously, it can be fun to let
oneself be surprised. The charm of this
technique lies in the running of the colours into each other, and the interest-
ing patterns that result from this.

I sometimes think for a long time about
a piece that I have vaguely in mind, how,
where and when, and by whom it is to
be worn, and how I can make the most
of the means at hand. If it is to be a pre-
sent for the home, how will the object's
colours match those of its future environ-
ment, or, if it is to be a piece of jewellery, which garment is it to match, and at
what time of day is it to be worn?

Necklace and ear-rings. "Gold" mixture poured into plastic bottle tops injected with light-blue opaque and blue translucent. Wrong side coated with "gold" mixture. Chain embedded.

4

PREPARATIONS

This material has a limited pot life. The exact time depends on the product and is invariably indicated in the directions. It is essential to adhere to the times indicated.

By and large, the material can be used in a free-running condition for about an hour. From that time on it becomes progressively tacky; the glass-clear mixture gels more quickly than those containing pigment. The material is workable for about 3 to 5 hours. The work should be arranged so that first the horizontal areas are covered. For vertical or moulded areas, the material should be thick-flowing and slightly tacky. For objects to be covered thickly, or with raised contours, the resin should be so tacky that it can be lifted with a spatula. If the material is to be shaped — and that too is possible — it should be left to stand till of the right consistency. The hands should be covered in Vaseline before working the mixture. If you have mixed the resin and are prevented from using it, say, by an unexpected caller, you can put it in the refrigerator where it will remain usable for twenty-four hours. Slight warming will return it to liquid form. Quick and successful results depend on the preparations before mixing; all tools and accessories should be at hand, all measuring, cutting and designing should have been completed.

It is a good idea to put out a few more blanks than you intend to work. If not enough resin has been mixed, it is not so easy to obtain exactly the same colour shade in another batch. The rule therefore is, to mix a little more rather than less, and if necessary coat a few extra pieces. Sometimes the excess material produces some very pretty small articles, for instance, ear-rings, cufflinks, pendants or brooches.

15

Pendants. Fashioned in clay or modelling compound, tooled and cured in a domestic oven. Coated with a variety of translucent colours.

Next to each pendant, a ring to match.

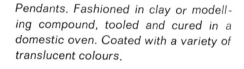

Colour plate:
The outlines of the design (for a mirror) were first drawn with a ball-point from a paper pattern. The lines were then retraced with a brush filled with "silver" mixture. The areas were filled in on the following day.

Brooch and ear-rings. Copper blanks covered with "silver" mixture. After gelling, apply a little glass-clear mixture at random, dust with "silver" powder. Finish off with green crystal-glass mosaic.

Colour Plate

Above left:
Wall mirror. Mirror, copper blanks and cardboard backing. Leaf shapes made from crumpled silver foil were stuck on to the copper blanks and covered light green, translucent. Last of all pre-cast dots, red opaque.

Underneath the mirror, on the right:
Brooch. Gilded blank covered with translucent blue as a ground. Next double-sided adhesive tape roughened and covered with resin and "gold" filler. When gelled it was lifted off and trimmed with scissors and then pressed on to the still tacky blue layer. Finished off with purple crystal-glass mosaic stones.

Left:
Pendant in two parts. Blanks partly covered with crumpled silver foil coated with translucent red and blue.
Immediately below:
Brooch. The shape was cut and covered on both sides with resin containing "silver" filler. Large circle opaque red, small circle glass-clear with light blue.

Bottom left:
Pendant. After shape had been cut out, it was covered on both sides with "silver" mixture. Inner shape covered with crumpled foil and coated with translucent purple, 3 drops glass clear, and one drop purple into each of these. Left to gel before being set in "silver" shape.

Top, right:
Brooch. Crumpled foil mounted on blank, coated light green, translucent. Finished off with glass clear, pre-cast dots.

Top, inside right:
Bracelet and brooch. Round shapes covered with translucent blue and red, injected with "gold" mixture. Jewellers' findings coated glass-clear. Stones mounted.
Brooch: Gilt metal blank coated glass clear, stone mounted.

Top half, centre:
Match-box cover. Stones made by coating home-made shapes. Individually mounted. Dark red transparent and yellow opaque.

Centre:
Pendant and bracelet. Metal blanks coated red opaque. Twenty-four hours later, yellow and white opaque dots were added.

Underneath:
Bracelet, heavily gilded. Designs painted in "silver" mixture with a brush, into each rectangle. Translucent blue coat superimposed.

Bottom right:
Small wooden box, bought unpolished from handicraft shop. The wood was stained dark-brown with boot polish. The lid was covered with silver foil. The "stones", home-made shapes coated with resin, were affixed with glass-clear mixture.

Bracelet, necklace and ear-rings. Blue mosaic crystals glued on. Coated translucent turquoise.

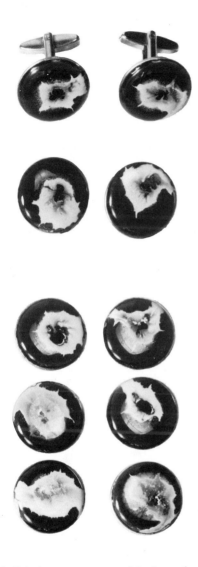

Cuff-links, ear-rings and buttons for a dress. Copper blanks coated translucent red, injected with drops of clear, opaque pink and translucent red.

Bracelet and belt buckle. Translucent yellow. Leave for twenty-four hours before adding black opaque.

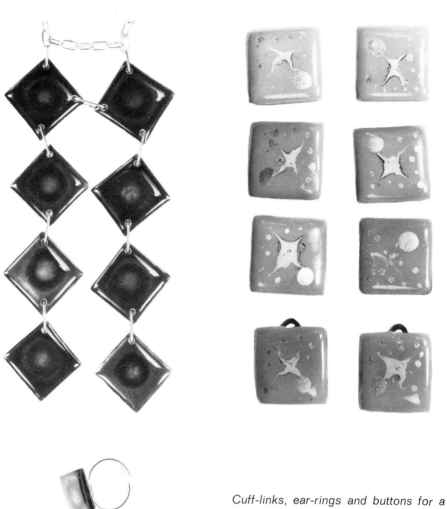

Cuff-links, ear-rings and buttons for a dress. Copper blanks coated opaque blue, with a few drops of glass-clear and gold mixture, to follow. One or two drawn out with a spatula.

Necklet, ear-rings and ring. "Stones" — resin on blank — translucent blue, green and purple, each with a few drops of the other two colours. Smooth silver foil embedded on reverse side.

Bangle. Bangle straightened, coated white and black opaque. Spirals drawn. After twenty-four hours, the bangle was bent back into shape. Brooch covered to match.

Hair slide and button-chain link. Circles superimposed. Dark-red translucent with light-red dots, opaque.

Curved bangle. Set with translucent blue and green dots, pre-cast in resin. Dots glued on.

Necklace. Copper blanks with mounted shapes of crumpled silver foil, coated transparent blue. Other side coated glass-clear. Pendants and chains embedded.

5

THE PIGMENTS

The larger the amount of pigment added to the prepared resin mixture, the more intense the colour tone. Excessive proportions of colour paste or metal filler are not recommended, however, as this greatly retards the gelling of the resin. The pigments should be well stirred in, so that they combine thoroughly with the resin. All materials, including the pigments, should be at room temperature before mixing. It makes for easier working if all ingredients have the same temperature.

It is advisable to add the pigment on completion of the pre-reaction time. Should the material have become tacky, gentle warming will restore it to its free-flowing state. The more free-flowing the material, the easier it is to mix in the pigments, and the fewer bubbles will form. It should be borne in mind that heating accelerates gelling, and it can in fact be used to shorten the setting time.

In order to obtain a pure opaque white, use the recommended maximum of white pigment, as otherwise the clear resin will show up as a slight blue shadow.

All pigments are intermixable so that every colour shade can be obtained.

If the colours are intended to run into each other, apply the mixture whilst free-flowing on top or next to each other. If the colour lines are to be clearly defined, one colour must be allowed to dry before the next is applied. The gelling times will be indicated in the directions supplied with the resin. Here again, heating may shorten the setting time. If contour lines have been drawn, these should be completely dry before the colour fields are filled in. Painting then, however, may be carried out in one operation as the dividing lines will prevent the colours from running into each other, whether opaque or translucent.

If any resin containing hardener clings to your spatula, be sure to wipe it clean before using it to remove pigment from a tin.

Cuff-links, gilded, with "brilliant" cut (having horizontal faces), coated transparent blue and green.

Coated golden yellow, translucent.

Cufflinks and earclips, formed over a template. The base is translucent red, then opaque pink, glass-clear drops, more clear red and a final coat of "gold". The findings are embedded and the underside finished with glass-clear.

Ear-rings and ornamental buttons, blue, leather. Indentations filled with "gold" mixture to which were added drops of glass-clear and translucent blue and red.

Brooch. Opaque red applied to copper blanks, with a dusting of "gold" powder.

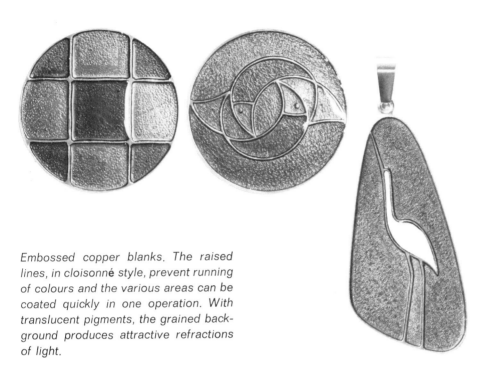

Embossed copper blanks. The raised lines, in cloisonné style, prevent running of colours and the various areas can be coated quickly in one operation. With translucent pigments, the grained background produces attractive refractions of light.

Ear-rings and buttons for HER — cuff-links and tie-pin for HIM. All coated translucent green and dusted with "gold" powder. A belt buckle that will go with them is on p. 44.
In order to ensure even coating, the blanks were pressed into Plasticine. This method should be followed in the case of all blanks that do not lie level.

Key ring: glass-clear over translucent red and blue.

Pocket mirrors. In the three round mirrors, the plastics frames had been removed and the reverse side and edges were coated. Above left: Light- and dark-green, translucent, with a dusting of "gold" powder. Above right: Coated with "gold" mixture and decorated with ornamental stones, in red, pink, purple and dark-purple. Bottom right: Translucent blue "stones" cast on blanks and mounted on "gold" mixture, finished with glass-clear coating.
Mirror with handle: Coated translucent blue and decorated with dark-red, light-red and yellow crystals.

6

THE BLANKS

In our sense, the word "blank" is not confined to the metal discs and shapes sold under that description but embraces anything that can be coated with synthetic resin.

Almost everything is suitable for resin-coating, with the exception of Plexiglass, thermoplastics, rubber and soft PVC (vinyl plastic). This leaves us with glass, china, stoneware, earthenware, wood, cardboard, paper, textiles, leather, stone and metal.

Blanks for jewellery and for small gift articles are obtainable from every handicraft store. Blanks intended for enamelling are sometimes supplied with a separate copper shape. This means two for the price of one; you can coat the cut-out area of the lid and use the copper inlay as a pendant, or a brooch.

It is also quite possible to cut one's own blanks from tin or metal foil, or copper or aluminium plate. Blanks may also be moulded. There are a number of modelling compounds now on the market which can be dried at room temperature or cured in a domestic oven (as well as fired in a kiln). Blanks may also be cut out of plywood or strong cardboard. Any of these as well as the wide variety of blanks on sale, may be turned into really attractive presents.

The one thing to remember in respect of all blanks is that they must be absolutely free from grease. Even a trace of grease will prevent the proper adhesion of the resin. Every blank should be wiped with methylated spirit.

Copper blanks intended for coating with translucent resin should first be cleaned with a good metal polish to give them an extra sparkle. This must be followed by another rubbing with methylated spirit, so that the polish does not provide an insulating agent.

Clock. Some handicraft shops stock
copper blanks divided into segments,
with battery-operated works to match,
to make a wall-clock. This clock was
coated two-tone blue, translucent, with
drops of glass-clear. Round portions
coated separately in translucent red
and mounted.

28

Wooden box. Blue metal foil was glued
to the lid, followed by beads, also glued.
A clear-glass coating was then applied.

The sides were treated with bronze-gold.

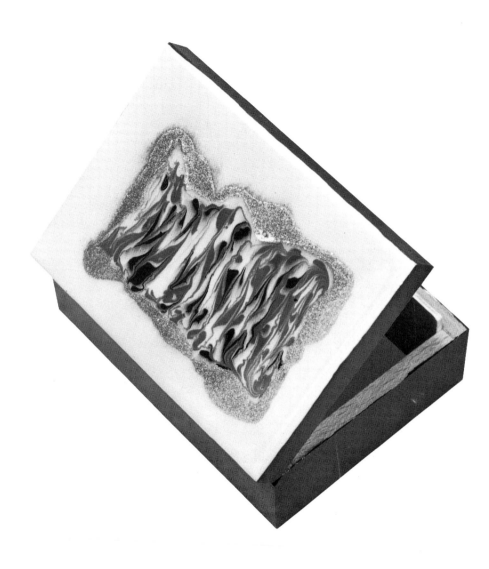

Cigarette box. The lid was coated with
opaque white, and opaque and translucent red were added in drops, then
drawn out with a darning needle. "Gold"
powder was sprinkled as a border. The
sides were stained red.

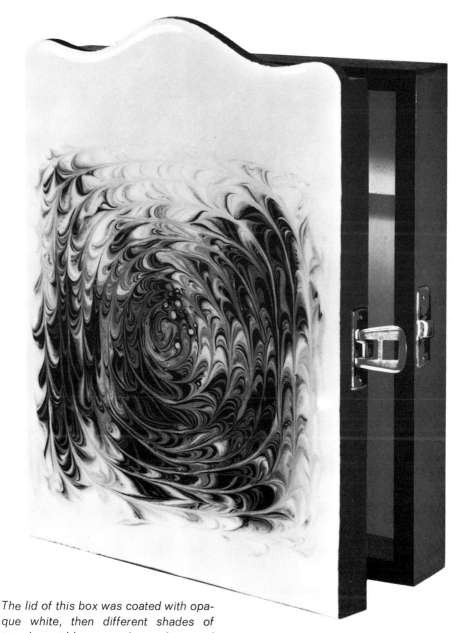

The lid of this box was coated with opaque white, then different shades of translucent blue were dropped on, and "gold" powder added. Spirals were trailed with a spatula. The sides were painted blue.

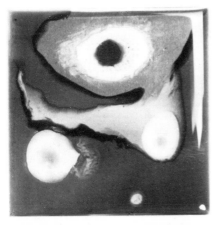

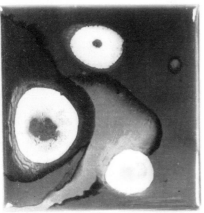

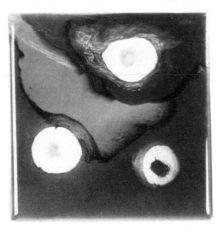

Copper tiles. For use as a stand or wall decoration, or for a narrow tray. Opaque white drops in various translucent shades of blue, red and yellow.

Colour plate:
Six ceramic tiles with widely different decoration. Each tile should be visualised on its own, as wall decoration or as a table stand. Or imagine several of the same design combined as a flower stand or a coffee table. These are only six of countless possibilities.

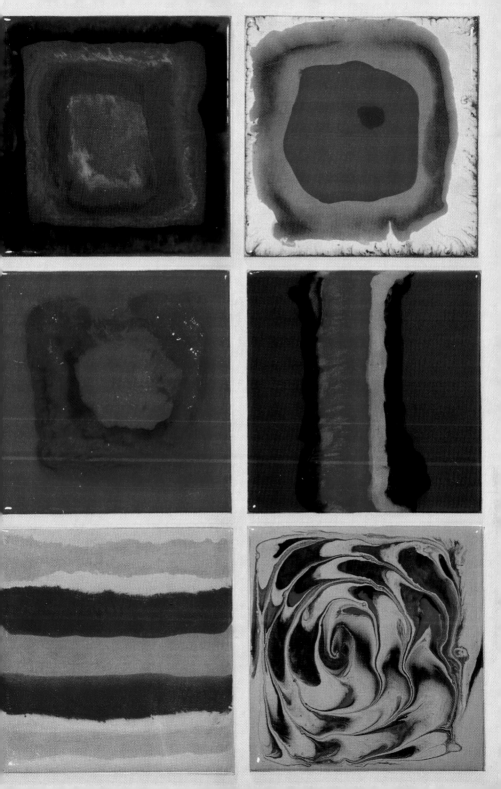

Colour Plate:
Three necklaces built up from very simple forms.

Window ornament. A pane of glass, bought ready cut, with smoothed edges, placed over paper design. Outlines traced with a brush, in translucent dark red. Areas were filled in the following day, in translucent yellow, orange, light-red and dark-red. Loops made by bending wire were fastened with glass-clear mixture. Suspended by a nylon thread.

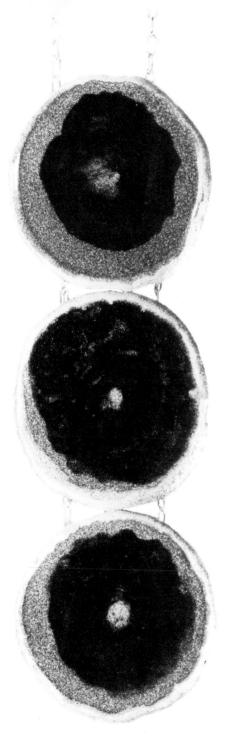

Depending on the size and number of discs, this design can be used for a window decoration, a room divider or a necklace. "Gold" mixture cast on a stencil, with added translucent blue, glass clear, translucent green and drops of "gold" mixture.

Owl. Wall decoration. The owl consists of curtain rings, nuts and nails, arranged on a piece of plywood, 20 x 30 cm, coated with "silver" mixture. Place curtain rings, nuts and nails before the resin has gelled, using tweezers. Next day fill in the areas with translucent mixture, red, turquoise, blue and yellow. Fix holder on reverse side.

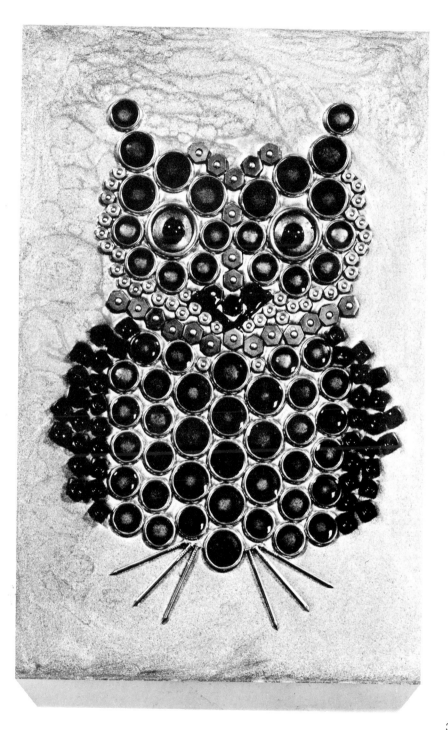

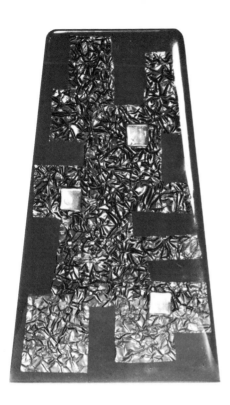

Ready-made bookends can be bought and decorated with shapes cut from crumpled foil plus some pieces of crystal glass in a contrasting colour. A clear coating can then be added.

7

THE WORK

Once the material has been mixed, it should be used quickly, regardless of attempts at interference or interruption. The proportion of catalyst and other materials may differ; the important thing is to follow the instructions provided with the resin. The success of the work depends on that. This may sound rather frightening but every housewife knows that careful weighing-out is essential for palatable results.

It may happen that too much catalyst, or hardener, has been poured into the measuring cup. If so, throw it away. Do not return it to the bottle.

If you buy a large tin of resin as a refill, transfer a small amount at a time to a small tin. The same applies to the hardener. It is easier to pour out exact amounts from small containers than from large ones.

Measuring cups should be cleaned immediately after use. Pour a little methylated spirit into the cups and wipe with a cloth or rag.

A rag soaked in methylated spirit should also be used to clean all tools,

the hands, and the blank or other object to be coated. Use the rag, which should be of a non-fluffy material, from one corner and roll it up a little more after every use. This will save your fingers from getting dirty. Note Methylated Spirit (methyl alcohol) is flammable — do not use near a naked flame, including lighted cigarettes.

To avoid getting resin on your fingers, hold the container securely in your hand, slightly inclined. Always scrape the spatula at the same place, and pour from the same place. After the pigment has been mixed into the clear mixture, leave for two or three minutes. The bubbles rise to the surface and can be moved to one side with a spatula. If bubbles have formed on the coated object, they can be burst with a spatula or a pin, or a dry brush may be drawn across the half-gelled material. When using a brush for coating (only with free-flowing material) draw it along; do not push it to and fro, this makes for bubbles. Brushes must be cleaned at once, before the resin sets.

Wall ornament or outdoor light. Lid of a polythene food container, 20 x 20 cm (8 x 8") filled with glass-clear mixture in which were placed glass marbles. As wall decoration: mount it on a 60 x 60 cm (24 x 24") wooden board, painted white. As outside lamp: have a wrought-iron case made to measure, painted black.

"Bird" and "Fish" wall ornaments. Have the outline made in wrought iron (the ends need not be soldered). Prepare pieces of coloured glass by wrapping glass in a thick cloth, then smashing. Cover the work-table with plastics sheet. Place the metal frame on this and pour in glass-clear resin. Then embed your glass and finish with another layer of glass-clear. Suspend from nylon cord.

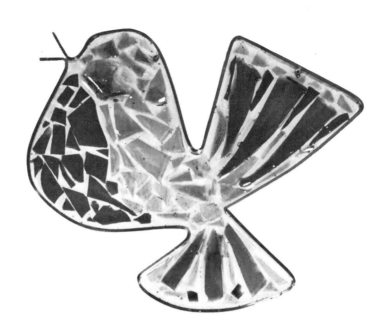

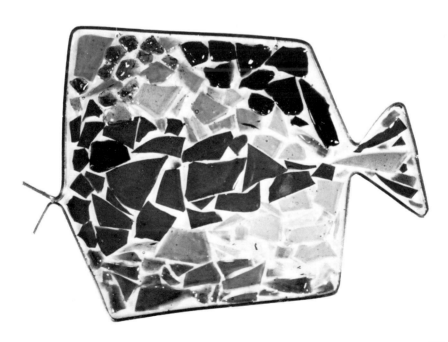

39

8

EFFECTS

The material is in itself effective enough, but with the confidence born of experience, it is fun to experiment.

Translucent colours may be allowed to intermingle, or a few drops of opaque may be injected into a translucent application, or "gold" or "silver" powder may be sprinkled on the resin coat before it has gelled.

A wide variety of embedded objects can look very attractive: pebbles, glass splinters, flowers, flower seeds, leaves and other plant portions, insects, tiny starfish, fish scales, shells, butterflies, metal parts, photographs, beads, crystals and mosaic stones, wire and even locks of hair.

Twenty-four hours after embedding, apply another coat of glass-clear to increase the lustre. This applies to coated objects as well.

For spiral effects, apply translucent and opaque colours (or only translucent or only opaque) to cover the area. Then take the spatula and draw a tight spiral, beginning in the centre.

Very pretty effects can be obtained by using silver foil (from chocolate or cigarette packets, as well as cooking foil) as background for translucent colours. Crumple the foil and smooth out again. It may either be used to cover the entire object to be coated, or in cut-out shapes (e. g. sailing boats, flowers, abstract forms). Metal foil may also be embossed and then coated.

If pebbles or crystal-glass stones are to be embedded, they must be fixed to the blank before the resin is poured on, as the impact would disperse them.

Raised dots are obtained by allowing half-gelled material to drip on to the base. The drops must be far enough apart to keep separate. When hard, lift off and place in position on the object before the top coat has gelled.

Every oil-free drawing on simple drawing paper, every photograph, every art print and every silhouette can be coated with clear mixture and become translucent.

Sometimes a colour print that would make a good transparency has printing on the reverse side, or the paper is too thick for translucency. In this case, the picture side is coated with glass-clear mixture and left to harden for two or three days. After that, it is soaked in water (containing a small amount of liquid detergent) until the softened paper may be rubbed away from the back. It is advisable to use a piece of chamois leather, or one's fingers can get very sore.

The remarkable thing is that the picture remains in the glass-clear mixture. After drying, the reverse side is coated; a fastener may be embedded or holes can be drilled later. You now have a transparency.

Textiles are coated on the right side — uses include lamp-shades and wall panels. The glass-clear resin seeps through and the character of the weave is preserved. For fabric coating, the table should always be covered with plastic foil so that when the resin has set, the piece can be easily removed.

For a matt surface, the coated object should be exposed to steam. The time to do this is when the mixture is no longer runny but the surface has not yet set hard. The longer the exposure to the steam, the more matt the surface. If it has become too dull, warm air (hair dryer) will restore the lustre.

A young leaf in the spring will become transparent if coated on both sides. The mature, more richly pigmented leaves of summer can no longer be made transparent. They may, however, be removed after the resin has hardened; the leaf structure will remain as a delicate relief. A dry leaf cannot be removed, not even if it has been coated only on one side.

Trinket box. Some glass-clear resin was dripped onto a sheet of rubber, left to solidify and then lifted off. The lid was coated with opaque white; "gold" and translucent red were added in drops, and the solid drops lightly pressed on. The sides were painted red.

Metal case for large matchbox. The mounted relief: Press a rectangle, about 1 cm (approx. ¹/₂") deep, into Plasticine. Into this mould, press an assortment of other shapes. Pour in light green mixture, translucent. When set hard, remove from Plasticine, scrub clean in soapy water, and coat with clear resin. Mount on metal case with glue.

Belt buckle. Coated translucent green and dusted with "gold" powder.

Cases for matchboxes and matchbooks. Coatings may be translucent, opaque or both. Small tumbled stones or crystalglass mosaic may be added as decoration.

Powder compact and three small boxes. Compact coated translucent blue, a drop of opaque red and a sprinkling of "gold" powder. Boxes, top to bottom: translucent green coat with light green opaque, glass-clear, light green opaque and the centre again translucent green. Translucent turquoise with opaque white, into that again translucent turquoise. Translucent red and blue, glass-clear, with pre-cast dots.

Cigarette case coated black and white opaque, with separately cast light-brown opaque dots.

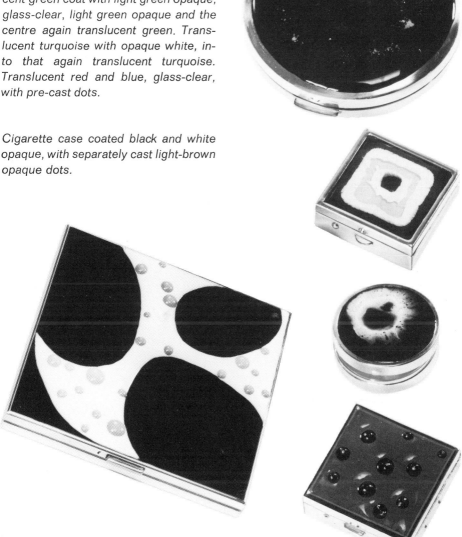

Examples of rubber templates

9

ACCESSORIES

I know I have said it before but I will say it again, almost anything can be coated with epoxy resin. We are by no means dependent on purchased blanks or templates. The material may also be cast on *silicone rubber stencils* and removed after setting.

The templates may be used over and over again. It is also possible to cut one's own rubber templates. I have used up an entire rubber bath mat for the purpose.

Free-flowing material will form a thinner coat than more viscous resin. It is advisable, some time after the first application, when the resin has become more tacky, to drop some more in the middle of the stencil to produce a thicker coating.

The plastics lids of margarine containers are useful for embedding objects to be used as window ornaments. The lettering must be covered with white plastics sheet, e. g. Con-tac.

Yoghurt containers and rubber stoppers make useful moulds.

Panes of glass can be bought cut to size and can then be coated. Metal framing for window transparencies is available from some handicraft shops. After the metal strip has been cut and bent to fit the drawing, it is placed on a rubber plate. The metal framing should be exactly in line with the edge of the plate before being affixed with plastic adhesive tape. Adhesion must be good; on the one hand the metal must not slip, and on the other hand, the mixture must not run out between frames and rubber plate. When all pieces of the frame are correctly in place, a clear coat is poured in to a thickness of $1/2$ mm ($1/64$"). The metal joints must also be filled in with clear resin to prevent intermingling of the colours. The individual colour areas can then be filled with resin to the edge of the frame, that is, after the clear base has set.

All the findings for ear-rings, cuff-links, brooches, necklaces and bracelets, as well as other fastenings, chains, buttons and blanks can be obtained from handicraft shops.

Wall candle-holder. Two pieces of ply-wood, shaped as shown. Sandpaper edges. Cut pattern into long strip of linoleum. Coat surface of lino-leum with silverbronze; over that apply resin coat, translucent blue. Fix lino to plywood. Smooth edges. Paint edges and small piece of plywood with some left-over blue oil paint. Drill hole in square piece for candleholder (obtain-able from handicraft shops). Screw in spiked candle-holder. Glue square un-derneath long piece. Fix picture hook on reverse side.

Candle-holders. Above left, coated blue translucent and white opaque, spirals drawn with spatula. Below left: Dividing lines drawn with a brush filled with "sil-ver" mixture. On following day, fields filled in with black and white opaque. Centre: Opaque light-turquoise with black in centre; black lines drawn from centre to edge with spatula. Above right: Coated translucent green, deco-rated with light-green and white crystal mosaic stones. Below right: Coated translucent blue; white opaque spirals painted with brush on the following day.

Large candle-holder: Coated translu-cent dark red. On following day: white opaque applied to edge and allowed to run.

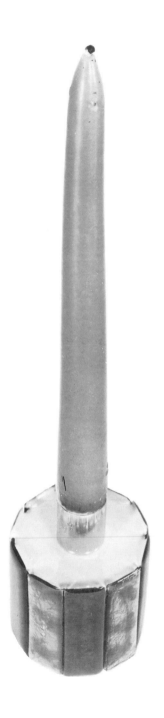

Egg-timer for telephone addicts. Rubber forms coated glass-clear, covered with crumpled silver foil, top coating of green or blue translucent, each with a few drops of the other colour.

Candlestick from an empty tin. Cover tin with crumpled metal foil and stick down. Cast "stones", light-green and dark-green translucent, on rubber forms cut to match. Insert top of a cosmetics bottle to do duty as candle-holder.

Pencil tray, letter opener and container for adhesive tape. Useful presents for anyone working in an office. Metal pencil tray (from stationers) coated translucent green. Embedded shapes, black and pink opaque, pre-cast on rubber stencils.

Letter opener: Handle coated all round in white opaque. "Stones", light-green and dark-green translucent, pre-cast over crumpled foil on cut-out rubber shapes, pressed into the white coating.

Container for adhesive tape: Leather trimming taken off, remains of adhesive removed with acetone. Coated blue opaque, red opaque and blue translucent.

Sculpture. A piece of driftwood, found on the beach and coated with "gold" mixture. The base: Translucent red, poured into a yoghurt container. When set, this was varnished with clear resin before the sculpture was mounted.

Vase made from a cardboard roll. Cut down a cardboard roll to the size required, block one end with a cardboard disc glued in. Cut a piece of copper sheeting to size, emboss and coat translucent blue. Line the inside of the tube by pouring in black opaque resin — which must be free-flowing — and rotating. Gently bend the copper foil and glue to the roll. Draw lines, using a brush, with black opaque mixture, half gelled. Use a spatula to coat the rim.

10

TRICKS OF THE TRADE

In time, one tends to discover one's own little dodges, but here are a few to be going on with: —

If resin has been applied too liberally, it will run over the edges of the stencil. In this case, remove some material, clean the edge (e. g. the border of a cuff-link) with a rag soaked in methylated spirit. Add some more resin when it has become more tacky.

Should dust particles have settled on the surface, leave to set and re-coat with clear mixture.

If material has been applied in a tacky state, so that the surface has set uneven, warm the object with a hair-dryer. This will liquefy the surface and cause it to run. It will then dry evenly.

For one day after gelling, resin may be cut with a knife or with scissors. If this leaves a ragged edge, coat with clear mixture.

Lino-cuts can be used to obtain relief effects. Paint the cut-out linoleum with oil before casting. When cutting, be sure not to produce undercuts as these would make it difficult to remove the cast.

If you are not sure how a particular colour will go with a given background, apply a test drop and remove immediately with a meth-soaked rag. You can then adjust the colour shade, either making it deeper by the addition of more pigment, or lighter with clear resin.

For raised layers, stick adhesive tape round blanks or templates. Remove after twenty-four hours. Trim the edges, file or sandpaper them, and coat them with clear mixture to make them smooth. Wait three or four days before drilling holes.

The affixing of brooch fasteners is very simple. Coat the entire reverse side of the "jewel" with $\frac{1}{2}$ mm ($\frac{1}{64}$") of resin. Bend the bar slightly outward so that, in pressing it into the resin, neither joint nor pin is covered. Use the spatula to apply another coat to the bar so that it is completely enclosed.

Vase made from bottle. Vessel covered with half-gelled, tacky mixture, strawberry opaque. Pre-cast dots, white opaque, mounted next day with glue.

Vase made from bottle. Bottle covered with half-gelled, tacky mixture, brown opaque. Next day, application of rose opaque mixture, again half-gelled and tacky.

54

Glass vase and boxes. Vase: Cut out forms and coat with translucent blue mixture. Next day, bend gently over finger and fix to glass with glue.

Box, left: Teak box with copper lid (handicraft shop). Copper wire turned into spirals with pliers and embedded in translucent blue coat.

Jar, right: Blue pottery jar. Design and cut out rubber form, coat with "gold" mixture, embed red synthetic gem stones. Fix to lid with glue.

Ashtrays and sweet-dishes. Scatter lump enamel in bottom of ashtray, cover with clear resin. Coat rim opaque red. Dish, bottom left: Coated blue translucent and white opaque; spirals drawn with spatula. Above: Dish coated dark red, light red and yellow translucent. Bottom right: Dish coated light blue opaque, finished off with pre-cast glass-clear droplets.

11

CLEANING

Perhaps the most vital accessory in resin work is methylated spirit. Always have a meth-soaked rag within reach, and you will not have sticky fingers.

Methylated spirit (methyl alcohol) should also be used to clean the tools immediately after use. Never forget — the spirit is highly flammable.

The rag or cloth soaked in methylated spirit is best kept in a container. This avoids damp areas on the working surface.

As the spatula will have to be constantly wiped, it is essential to have a non-fluff producing cloth at one's elbow.

Fold over as required, so as to avoid contact with wiped off resin.

Clean the measuring cups immediately after use. Otherwise the remains of resin in the bottom will harden and the marks will no longer be accurate.

It is a good idea to apply a barrier cream to the hands before commencing work. This makes them much easier to clean afterwards.

If a mishap does occur, and a drop of resin has got on to your clothes, sponge immediately with methylated spirit. Up to twelve hours you may get it out, after that it is hopeless. Moral: wear clothes that don't matter.

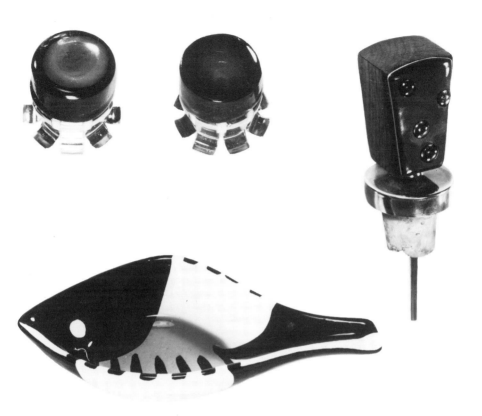

Ceramic dishes. Coat basic form with opaque layer. When set, decorate with translucent or opaque colours. Bold designs are suitable for this technique.

Ornamental cork. Wooden form coated translucent green, with injection of opaque yellow.

Wooden shape covered turquoise opaque. Thread enamel placed on surface.

Transparent mixture poured onto rubber stoppers. After gelling, they were coated with clear resin and mounted on bottle tops.

Copper blank on wooden form, coated blue and green translucent. Finished off with glass clear, pre-cast droplets.

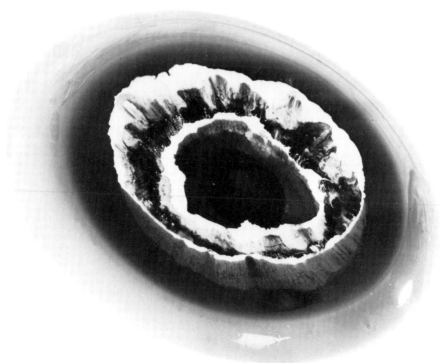

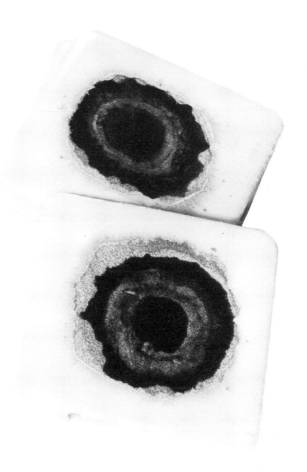

Plate. A damaged piece from the kitchen. Coated blue translucent with an inner circle of light-blue opaque with clear and more translucent blue in the centre.

Tile stands. Cast on pieces of cardboard. light-blue opaque, infiltrate "gold" mixture, glass-clear, green translucent, glass-clear, "gold" mixture, green translucent.

Above: Tile coated light-blue opaque. Drops of "gold" mixture, into these, light-green translucent drops. Drawn out with a spatula.

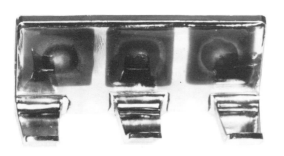

Coat-hook. A round stone, green translucent with strip of turquoise opaque,
mounted on plate coated with glass-
clear mixture.

Towel rail. Three stones cast on stencils in translucent green, blue and purple shades, mounted on strip coated with
glass-clear resin mixture.

Door knob and knob for drawer. Door
knob: Blue translucent, infiltrated with
yellow opaque. Knob for drawer: Blue
and green translucent.

12

AN A B C
OF THE POSSIBILITIES

A	Art work, ashtrays
B	Bangles, bottle labels, bracelets, brooches, buckles and buttons
C	Candlesticks, clips, cocktail sticks, coffee tables, containers, cuff-links
D	Diary covers, door knobs, drawings
E	Ear-rings, embedding
F	Family crests, fancy goods, flower tables, fruit bowls
G	Garden ornaments, gifts
H	Hair ornaments, house numbers
I	Icons, insects (for embedding)
J	Japanning, jars, jewellery, jewel cases
K	Kitchenware
L	Lamp bases and shades, lanterns
M	Maps, matchbox cases, mobiles, mosaics
N	Napkin rings, necklaces
O	Ornaments
P	Paper-weights, pendants, photographs, powder compacts
Q	Quince seeds, arranged and embedded
R	Repairs, rings
S	Sign posts, snuff-boxes, stones
T	Tableware, tiles, tins, transparencies, trays
U	Umbrella stands
V	Vanity cases, vases
W	Wall decorations, wastepaper baskets, window ornaments, wooden boxes
X	Xmas decorations
Z	Zip fastener pendants